DATE DUE   APR 0 7

GAYLORD   PRINTED IN U.S.A.

Rattlesnakes

Other titles in the Nature's Predators series include:

NATURE'S PREDATORS

Rattlesnakes

Deanne Durrett

KIDHAVEN
PRESS™

THOMSON

GALE

San Diego • Detroit • New York • San Francisco • Cleveland
New Haven, Conn. • Waterville, Maine • London • Munich

© 2004 by KidHaven Press. KidHaven Press is an imprint of The Gale Group, Inc., a division of Thomson Learning, Inc.

KidHaven™ and Thomson Learning™ are trademarks used herein under license.

For more information, contact
KidHaven Press
27500 Drake Rd.
Farmington Hills, MI 48331-3535
Or you can visit our Internet site at http://www.gale.com

LIBRARY OF CONGRESS CATALOGING-IN-PUBLICATION DATA

Durrett, Deanne, 1940-
  Rattlesnakes / By Deanne Durrett.
    p. cm. — (Nature's Predators)
  Summary: Discusses the physical characteristics, habitat, and behavior of rattlesnakes, including how they hunt and kill.
  Includes bibliographical references and index.
    ISBN 0-7377-1889-7 (alk. paper)
    1. Rattlesnakes—Juvenile literature. [1. Rattlesnakes. 2. Snakes.] I. Title. II. Series.
  QL666.O69D87 2004
  597.96'38—dc22
                                                            2003016249

Printed in the United States of America

CONTENTS

CHAPTER ONE

Respected Predator

When the first explorers and settlers came to America, they found a snake that did not exist in Europe. Since the snake had a rattle at the end of its tail, they called it a rattlesnake. When disturbed or threatened, the rattlesnake vibrates its tail and makes a warning sound. Some people compare the sound to dry leaves rustling in a strong breeze. Others think it sounds more like a Spanish dancer's castanets.

About thirty species of rattlesnakes live in the Americas. The western diamondback is the best known of all rattlesnakes. This rattler has the widest range, delivers more bites, and has been made famous in Western movies. Other species include the largest, the eastern diamondback (six feet long or more). Because of its size, its bite is the most deadly. The ridge-nosed rattlesnake is the smallest (about twelve inches).

Rattlesnakes vary in color depending on the variety and the stage of mote (skin shedding). Most rattlesnakes are combinations of several colors including brown, tan, yellow, gray, black, white, red, and olive green. Species are identified by their size, color, and markings, which include diamond, chevron, or blotched shapes on their backs and sides. Some have stripes on

Some Species of Rattlesnake

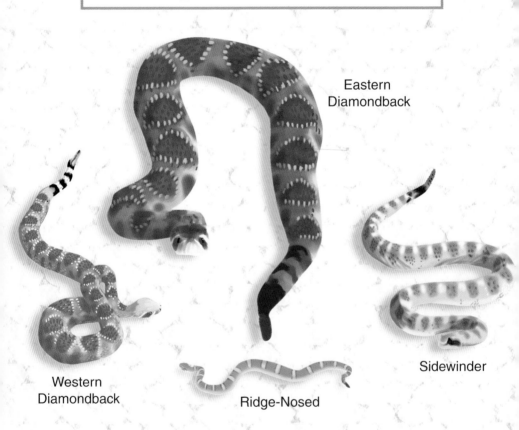

Eastern
Diamondback

Sidewinder

Western
Diamondback

Ridge-Nosed

their head and tail. The rattlesnake's color and markings help it blend in with its natural surroundings and become almost invisible. This is ideal for a creature that lays in wait to ambush prey.

New World Vipers

All rattlesnakes belong to the Viperidae family, more commonly known as vipers. There are two branches of the Viperidae family. Old World vipers (Viperinae) live in Europe, Asia, and Africa. New World pit vipers (Crotalinae) live in the Americas. These include the copperhead, cottonmouth water moccasin, and rattlesnake. (These three pit vipers plus the coral snake are the four deadly poisonous snakes found in the United States.)

Nature has equipped the rattlesnake and other pit vipers with a unique set of senses. Pit vipers have heat-sensing organs called loreal pits. These forward-facing pits are located between the eye and nostril on each side of the snake's flat triangular head. The loreal pits send heat images to the snake's brain. These images combine with normal eyesight to give the snake day and night vision.

Rattlesnake Country

Rattlesnakes live in an area that extends from southern Canada to northern Argentina and Uruguay. Fifteen species of rattlesnakes, including the western diamondback and sidewinder, live in the United States. At least one species can be found in each of the lower forty-eight states except Maine and Delaware. The

Fifteen species of rattlesnakes live in the United States. The western diamondback (pictured) is the best known of all rattlesnakes.

southwestern United States is home to the largest number of rattlesnakes. Eleven species can be found in Arizona alone.

Rattlesnakes live in areas where rodents are abundant, including the plains, deserts, forests, and mountains. They like rough terrain with bushes and rocks that provide hiding places for ambushing prey. They also need a place where they can find protection from the sun, shelter from the cold, and a safe place to **hibernate**.

People have moved into rattlesnake territory, clearing farmland and building homes. Rattlesnakes are attracted to prey that can be found in urban as well as rural areas. These include parks, campgrounds, new housing developments, and golf courses.

The Menu

Rattlesnakes are **carnivorous**. Scientists learn what snakes eat by observing the snake or examining snake **scat**. They look for identifiable hair, bones, and teeth the snake could not digest. Rattlesnakes choose their prey to match their size. A young rattler can only swallow prey such as centipedes, small lizards, and mice. Some species eat only warm-blooded mammals including mice, rats, squirrels, prairie dogs, and

A western diamondback devours a mouse. Rattlesnakes choose prey to match their size.

rabbits. Other species eat small rodents plus centipedes, lizards, and birds. Some have been known to eat young chickens and eggs. Rattlesnakes are good swimmers, and they occasionally eat fish.

When Rattlesnakes Eat

Rattlesnakes do not need to eat every day. They are not very active and have a slow **metabolism**. Some scientists think that the large eastern diamondback may be able to survive on two or three big meals a year. When food is plentiful, however, the snake eats five or six times a year.

Conditions must be right for a rattlesnake to eat. The snake eats only when it is warm enough and not too hot. And after a meal, it does not eat again until the swallowed prey is fully digested. Digesting a large rabbit may take two weeks. A rattlesnake does not eat during hibernation or until its body has had time to warm in the spring.

Cold-Blooded Creatures

Rattlesnakes are cold-blooded reptiles and do not produce their own body heat. They are most active when the temperature is between seventy and ninety degrees Fahrenheit. When the temperature rises above ninety-five degrees, a rattlesnake can die from heat exposure in a few minutes. When temperatures drop below sixty degrees, the rattlesnake is too sluggish to capture prey or defend itself. Consequently, rattlesnakes must seek shelter to survive in hot or cold weather.

A red diamond rattlesnake suns itself on some rocks. Rattlesnakes cannot produce their own body heat.

Where winters are mild, a rattlesnake will seek shelter in a crevice between rocks, among tree roots, or in another animal's shallow burrow. On warm days, the rattlesnake will come out to sun.

Where winters are severe, rattlesnakes hibernate below ground. Loners at other times, rattlers hibernate together in severe cold. Sometimes hundreds cluster in dens deep in the earth to **conserve** heat.

Rattlesnakes wake slowly from winter sleep, coming out to bask in the sun during the day and returning to shelter on cool nights. It may take as long as a month for the snake to warm, become fully active, and become hungry enough to hunt. During the ambush season (the warm months when rattlers hunt), the adult female rattlesnake must eat enough to gain body fat before she can produce a litter of young.

Live Bearers

Female rattlesnakes produce offspring every two to three years, depending on the species. Rattlesnakes are considered live bearers. Bearing young alters the female's feeding pattern. She will eat often before producing eggs. While she is **gravid** (carrying eggs) she may not eat at all. After the young are born, she will eat often and begin storing fat to see her through the next gestation period.

A rattlesnake gives birth. Rattlesnakes give birth every two to three years.

The birth process, however, is different from that of mammals. The female produces eggs that remain within her body until they are ready to hatch. Then the young emerge from her body as a live birth. Depending on the species, there may be as few as six or as many as twenty-one in the batch, ranging in size from six to fifteen inches. Newborn rattlers stay near their mother until they shed their first skin.

The youngster sheds its first skin within ten days of birth. It molts, or outgrows and sheds its skin, several times the first year. The rattler forms its first rattle after the first molt. It takes two rattle segments, however, to make sound. The young snake cannot rattle until the second molt.

The Rattles

A rattlesnake's rattles are actually two rows of jointed hollow buttons. A pair of new buttons (segments) is added each time the snake sheds its skin. Mature snakes molt only once or twice a year.

The rattles are made of dried skin called keratin (material similar to fingernails). Like fingernails, the segments of the rattle become brittle and break at times. Therefore, the idea that a snake's age can be determined by counting the rattles is a myth.

A rattlesnake can shake its rattles as fast as sixty times per second (about the average beat of hummingbird wings in normal flight). The buttons vibrate against each other creating the warning sound.

The rattling snake may be coiled or on the move. Most of the time, however, the rattles are quiet. The

Rattlesnakes can shake their rattles as fast as sixty times per second. Rattlesnakes do not always rattle before striking.

snake is shy and prefers to avoid people. Contrary to what most people think, rattlesnakes do not always rattle before striking. When human or animal feet come too close, the snake will defend itself and may strike without warning. The predator, however, never rattles before striking an ambushed prey. It silently waits. Coiled among leaves and twigs under a low bush, the rattlesnake is almost invisible—**camouflaged** and ready for quick action.

CHAPTER TWO

Ambush Season

Rattlesnakes are ambush hunters. They do not chase their prey. They wait and ambush their prey. Their hunting season is sometimes called ambush season.

Compared to its prey, the rattlesnake may seem to be at a disadvantage. While mice, rats, and other rodents dart about on legs, the rattlesnake crawls on its belly. Most of the snake's skeleton consists of ribs connected to its backbone with ball-and-socket joints (like the human hip). Each rib is attached to a scale on the snake's belly. By hooking the ground with the scales and pushing backward with its ribs, the snake glides smoothly along the ground, under brush, and over rocks. A race between a mouse and a snake would be something like a race between an SUV and a tank. The SUV is much faster. The tank is slower but hard to stop. Once the tank is in position

A timber rattlesnake crawls across a log. Rattlesnakes use their ribs and the scales on their bellies to move.

for attack, however, it is equipped to win. So is the rattlesnake.

The Ambush Site

Once a rattlesnake warms in spring, it leaves its winter shelter and searches for an ambush site. Rattlesnakes seldom venture far from their shelter. They return there for safety from predators and protection from the heat throughout the ambush season. The rattlesnake will winter in the same shelter year after year.

Natural camouflage and patience help the rattlesnake capture prey. The rattlesnake will choose an ambush site where it can blend in with the surroundings. The cold-blooded creature also needs protection from the hot sun. (When temperatures are too high or too low, the snake leaves the ambush site and returns to its shelter.) Suitable sites include a hiding place near the base of a low bush, among tree roots, or beside a fallen log. There is one more important requirement—the snake must find a place where it is likely to find prey.

Jacobsen's Organ

The rattlesnake, like other snakes, has a forked tongue. The snake constantly flicks its tongue in and out of its mouth. The snake is collecting scent molecules and delivering them to the Jacobsen's organ in the roof of its mouth. The Jacobsen's organ is an extraordinary scent detector that helps the snake locate mice and rabbit trails.

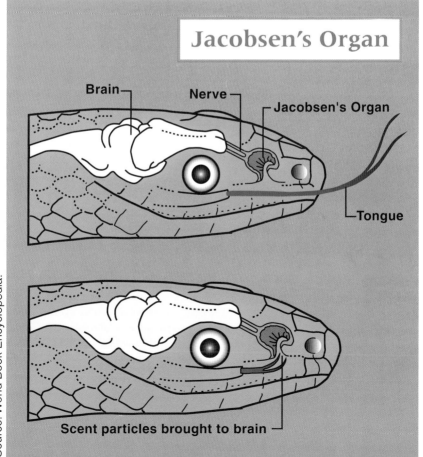

Jacobsen's Organ

Brain
Nerve
Jacobsen's Organ
Tongue
Scent particles brought to brain

Source: World Book Encyclopedia.

Once a trail has been detected, the snake looks for a hiding spot, curls its body into a coil, and waits. Prey that comes within striking distance is not likely to escape.

While rattlesnakes do not have ears, their whole body feels ground vibrations. They feel the movement as other creatures hear sound. This alerts them to the size and speed of an approaching prey or predator. In addition, rattlesnakes have a dual vision system that enables them to pinpoint their target.

Dual Vision

The rattler's eyes and loreal pits are both involved in sighting prey. Rattlesnakes have catlike eyes with slit

Rattlesnakes use both their eyes and heat sensors called loreal pits to see.

pupils. These pupils almost close in daylight and open wide at night. Their eyesight can detect movement. The snake's brain also receives information from its loreal pits. The snake's heat and light sensors focus on the same area. As a result, the snake sees an image created from both light and heat. So, its sight is not entirely dependent on light alone, allowing it to target prey at night.

The loreal pits can detect a difference in surface heat as small as .003 degrees Fahrenheit. Amazingly selective, the sensors ignore temperature readings from sources that stay in one place (such as a sun-warmed rock) and track a moving heat source (such as a mouse). In fact, a rattlesnake can detect the hot spot of its prey and direct its strike to the body mass near the heart rather than the head or limbs.

The snake strikes the instant prey comes within range (one-third to one-half the length of the snake's body). In less than half a second—faster than the human eye can follow—the rattlesnake lunges from its coil, strikes, releases the prey, and returns to its coil.

CHAPTER THREE

The Kill

Once it strikes, the rattlesnake does not hurry after its prey or watch where it goes. It relaxes and waits for the venom to kill. This is part of the rattlesnake's natural defense. The slow-moving rattlesnake cannot avoid a rodent's bite. It could be severely injured or killed in a physical tangle with its prey. Fortunately, the rattlesnake's natural instinct is to wait while the venom prepares its meal and then follow the trail. It can easily follow the trail to dead prey with its forked tongue and Jacobsen's organ.

Swallowing Prey

Many rattlesnakes swallow prey that equals up to half their body mass. Large rattlers, such as the diamond-backs, are capable of swallowing prey that equals twice their body mass. Sometimes the rattlesnake finds that it has tackled a prey that is too large. In this case the snake abandons its meal and prepares to ambush another prey.

When the rattlesnake reaches its kill, it slips its jaws out of joint, opens its mouth incredibly wide, and begins to swallow its meal whole. By this time, the venom (which is also a digestive juice) has begun

A western massasauga rattlesnake prepares to strike. After striking, rattlesnakes wait for their venom to kill the prey.

A timber rattlesnake swallows a deer mouse. Rattlesnakes swallow prey head first.

breaking down the prey's tissue. This predigestion makes the prey easier to swallow.

The snake takes the prey's head first and then works the body down its throat with teeth that have a backward curve. The prey will fill its throat for some time. In other creatures this would prevent breathing. The rattlesnake, however, has a tube in the bottom of its mouth that allows it to breathe while swallowing prey. The snake has no teeth for chewing or tearing chunks from its prey.

It may take several hours to swallow large prey. Meanwhile the rattlesnake is completely defenseless. After the snake has worked the prey past its mouth and down its throat, the snake will have a visible bulge in its body. Digestion may take several days depending on the size of the snake and the prey.

When the snake swallows a meal, its organs expand to aid in digestion. Some snakes, in fact, double the size of their intestines within twenty-four hours of swallowing prey.

While the snake is digesting a meal, it is slow and inactive. The warmth of the sun speeds up the digestive process. The sluggish snake, however, is vulnerable to predators. It will seek a hiding place while digesting its meal. If possible, it will make its way to its winter shelter and remain there until the meal is completely digested.

When the digestive process is complete, the snake will leave its shelter and find another ambush site. It will wait until prey approaches and then use its extremely efficient killing tools.

Retractable Fangs

The fangs are hollow and sharp, like a hypodermic syringe used by medical personnel. The opening is a slit along the side near the point. In this location, the opening does not clog with tissue as the fangs sink into the prey.

Fang length of mature snakes varies depending on the species. The longest fangs, measuring more than one-half inch, belong to the western diamondback. The snake does not use the fangs to tear the prey's flesh or chew. The fangs puncture the prey and inject venom.

When they are not in use, the fangs fold against the roof of the snake's mouth, sheathed in protective tissue something like a cat's claw is. During a strike, the hinged fangs spring forward and lock firmly in place as the snake fully opens its mouth. On contact, the fangs sink into the prey's flesh. As the rattlesnake releases the prey and pulls itself back into coil position, its fangs fold back into the roof of its mouth.

One or both fangs sometimes break during the quick strike and immediate release of the prey. Nature, however, has equipped the rattlesnake with replaceable fangs. A row of new fangs develop and grow behind each fang currently in use. When one fang breaks or falls out, a replacement moves into place. Old fangs are routinely shed and replaced several times a year. As a result, the rattlesnake always has a set of sharp fangs to deliver its venom.

Venom

Venom is created and stored in a gland at the base of each fang. The venom glands are located on each side of the snake's head, between the mouth and eye. When

When not in use, rattlesnake fangs are folded against the roof of the mouth (pictured). During a strike, the fangs spring forward and lock in place.

the snake bites, pressure on the glands forces venom through the fangs and into the prey (or enemy).

Once the venom glands are emptied, the snake will go hungry until it can produce more venom. A large western diamondback can produce about one-fourth

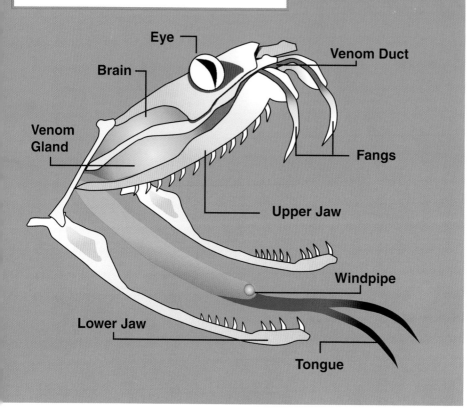

Eye

Brain

Venom Duct

Venom Gland

Fangs

Upper Jaw

Windpipe

Lower Jaw

Tongue

teaspoon every two weeks. For this reason, a mature rattlesnake does not inject the same amount of venom in each strike. It tries to conserve as much venom as it can. For example, a rattlesnake may inject no venom in a defense strike. This is a dry bite. When the snake is coming out of hibernation, its glands are full and it is too sluggish to escape a threat. At this time, it is likely to defend itself with a large dose of venom.

A rattlesnake strikes an animal that it knows is too big for it to swallow only to defend itself. Most of the time when humans are bitten they have accidentally stepped too close or were careless in handling a snake. Large animals become a threat when they step too close or poke a nose too near a rattler's hiding place.

Scientists do not know how much venom a rattlesnake injects during a strike. They do know, however, that the **lethal** dose of western diamondback venom is two to eight milligrams for each kilogram of body weight.

Drops of venom fall from the fang of a prairie rattlesnake. Once the venom glands are empty, rattlesnakes go hungry until more venom is produced.

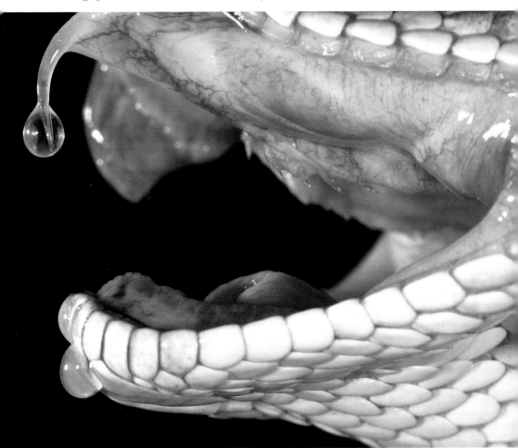

Rattlesnake venom is a combination of deadly **toxins** (poisons) that attack three ways. Any one of these toxins would be fatal to most prey. Some toxins attack the circulatory system, causing uncontrollable internal bleeding within six minutes. Other toxins attack the nervous system, paralyzing muscles including those that control breathing, the limbs, and heart. Other toxins attack the cells and break down the tissue. In fact, while making the kill, the venom begins digesting the snake's meal before it is swallowed.

While the rattlesnake digests its meal, it is vulnerable to attack from human and natural predators. It has little defense beyond camouflage and its frightening rattle. Its venom and strike are useless against some predators.

CHAPTER FOUR

Rattlesnake Predators

Rattlesnakes are most vulnerable to predators when they are young, swallowing and digesting prey, or gravid. However, whenever humans are near, rattlesnakes are vulnerable.

Small rattlesnakes and the young of all species fall prey to many predators. In fact, only a small percentage survive the first year.

Newborn western diamondbacks are about as big around as a pencil and only a few inches longer. Hawks, roadrunners, owls, and wild turkeys all prey on small snakes. Birds and animals that eat snakes are **ophiophagous**.

Roadrunners

One of the rattlesnake's most aggressive predators, the roadrunner, is packed with energy and speed. The bird, a member of the cuckoo family, eats young and

Roadrunners are the rattlesnake's most aggressive predators. Rattlesnakes are most vulnerable when they are young.

small snakes. It can fly only a few feet and attacks its prey from the ground. During an attack, the bird will dive and jump back. It uses its wings as a shield to protect its body from injury. In an attack on a rattlesnake, the bird makes a grab (usually for the tail) with its beak and moves back quickly. The roadrunner attacks repeatedly, and the snake tires. Then it grabs the snake by the tail and flings the snake from side to side. This pounds the snake's head against the ground. When the snake is dead, the roadrunner swallows it whole. It may take some time for the bird to swallow the snake. Roadrunners, however, are seldom still, and the bird can finish as it continues on its way.

Predator Snakes

Indigo and king snakes are ophiophagous. Like the roadrunner, these predators are immune to rattlesnake venom.

The king snake does not actively hunt rattlesnakes. When the two meet, however, the king snake will try to eat the rattlesnake (unless it is too large).

The rattlesnake is not an easy prey to capture. It detects the king snake as it nears and senses danger.

A king snake bites down on the head of a red rattlesnake. Although the king snake does not actively hunt rattlesnakes, it will attack a rattlesnake if the two meet.

The rattlesnake prepares to defend itself by lowering and flattening its head against the ground and raising a loop of its body. It swings the loop from side to side to block the king snake's attack. Meanwhile, the king snake tries to bite and grasp the rattlesnake near its head. If successful, this grip renders the rattlesnake helpless. The king snake then coils itself around its prey and squeezes. The rattlesnake cannot breathe, and dies.

The indigo snake also preys on rattlesnakes. This snake is large (six to seven feet in length) and strong. Indigo snakes attack and exhaust their prey. When the rattlesnake can fight no more, the indigo snake swallows it head first and alive. The prey, however, has taken its last breath when its head enters the predator's mouth. The rattlesnake appears to thrash about until most of its body is swallowed. Much of this movement may result from the indigo snake's effort to swallow. Some of it may be reflex action that occurs after the snake dies.

Fear of Snakes

Many people are afraid of snakes. They want to protect themselves by killing every snake they see. As a result, snakes of all kinds are hacked to death every year with any tool that is handy—shovels, hoes, and even golf clubs. Most snakes, however, are completely harmless. All snakes do far more good than harm. They help to control the disease-carrying rat and mouse populations. And, rattlesnakes are not aggressive toward people.

A sidewinder rattlesnake gazes straight into the camera.
Rattlesnakes are not aggressive toward people.

Researchers have tracked rattlesnakes with equipment such as radio transmitters and microchips. They found that when people come near, rattlesnakes often remain still and unseen. Other times, the snake slips away unnoticed. Most of the time when people encounter rattlesnakes, the snake is sunning after hibernation, digesting a meal, or on the way back to its winter shelter. At these times, the snake may be sluggish and unable to get away quickly. When a snake feels threatened, it will rattle its warning. If its warning is ignored, it will strike. Most bite victims, however, are careless snake handlers or hunters trying to capture the snake.

Rattlesnake Roundups

Annual rattlesnake roundups are held in Pennsylvania, Oklahoma, Texas, Kansas, Georgia, Alabama, and New Mexico. Okeene, Oklahoma, claims to have created the rattlesnake roundup around 1940.

Sportsmanship and ethics are not a part of rattlesnake hunting. The snakes are pulled from dens during hibernation, and many females are gravid. Many hunters use gasoline to force the snakes from the dens. This is cruel to the snakes. In addition, it ruins the area for all creatures and contaminates the groundwater.

The early roundups were intended to decrease the rattlesnake population and protect people living in the area from snakebite. Now, however, annual roundups have developed a carnival atmosphere with rides, talent shows, parades, and swap meet vendor booths. Unfortunately, most snake roundups have become festivals where snakes suffer incredible cruelty.

The captured rattlesnakes are dumped into a pit and displayed at the roundup. Later, people watch as the rattlesnakes are milked, sometimes skinned

A rattlesnake hunter holds the head of a rattlesnake during a rattlesnake roundup in Okeene, Oklahoma. Annual roundups are held in several states.

Snake handlers open a box filled with rattlesnakes in preparation for races at the World Championship Rattlesnake Races in Texas.

An albino western diamondback rattlesnake rests its head on its rattle. Rattlesnake skin is made into boots and hat bands.

alive, and beheaded. The snakes are sliced, fried, and served on a platter to anyone who wants to taste rattlesnake meat. Their skin is made into hat bands and boots, and the rattles are used for jewelry.

Many people consider rattlesnakes a worthless nuisance. Every creature on Earth, however, has value.

A Link in the Food Chain

The rattlesnake, both predator and prey, is a link in the food chain and plays an important role in the ecosystem. In the future it may play a priceless role in saving human life. Researchers think rattlesnake venom may someday provide treatments or cures for a variety of illnesses including cancer, arthritis, diabetes, and others. Unfortunately, these medicines may never be available. Some species of rattlesnakes are nearing extinction.

Today, several rattlesnake species are on state endangered lists, and timber rattlesnakes no longer exist in Canada, Delaware, Maine, and Rhode Island. Fortunately, the Humane Society and other protective organizations are taking steps to keep this valuable predator from extinction.

GLOSSARY

camouflage: The ability to blend into the surrounding area.

carnivorous: Eats meat.

conserve: To save or prevent waste.

gravid: Carrying unborn young (pregnant).

hibernate: To sleep through the winter.

lethal: Deadly.

metabolism: Bodily process that changes food to energy and controls the use of energy.

ophiophagous: Eats snakes.

scat: Fecal droppings.

toxins: Poisons.

FOR FURTHER EXPLORATION

Books

Bianca Lavies, *The Secretive Timber Rattlesnake.* New York: E.P. Dutton, 1991. This book is a photo essay that covers the life cycle of the timber rattlesnake, which is now on the endangered-species list.

Manny Rubio, *Rattlesnake: Portrait of a Predator.* Washington, D.C.: Smithsonian Institution Press, 1998. This book covers everything you might want to know about rattlesnakes and includes outstanding color photos.

Periodicals

Ellen Lambeth, "Rattlers! The Truth Is Told About the Amazing Rattlesnake," *Ranger Rick* vol. 32, May 1, 1998. This question-and-answer article covers many of the first questions that come to mind about rattlesnakes.

D. Bruce Means, "Snake Charmer," *National Wildlife* vol. 37, February 1, 1999. Written by an ecologist, this article covers the experience of a researcher studying the eastern diamondback rattlesnake. It includes how the snakes were tracked and information about the eastern diamondback.

Websites

American International Rattlesnake Museum (www.rattlesnakes.com). This website offers information and photos of rattlesnakes, plus illustrations that show how fangs and rattles work.

Desert USA (www.desertusa.com). This site offers information about roadrunners.

Natural Toxins Research Center (http://ntri.tamuk. edu/herpetarium/viperidae/c.atrox/milking.html). This site shows a rattlesnake milking demonstration.

Wonder Valley Ranch (http://wondervalleyranch. com/rattlesnakes.htm). This site offers information about three rattlesnake species found in the Mojave Desert, how to avoid snakes, and first aid for snakebite.

INDEX

PICTURE CREDITS

ABOUT THE AUTHOR

Deanne Durrett is the author of nonfiction books for young people from third grade to high school. She writes on many subjects and finds research and learning exciting. Durrett grew up in rattlesnake country, and her mother told her at an early age to "always look before you step." She now lives in a retirement resort community in Arizona with her husband, Dan. She still follows her mother's advice and looks before she steps. You can visit her website at www.deannedurrett.com.